Contents

A guide to this book

What will I learn?

In the next few chapters you will learn how to use two different programming languages. The first language is called **Scratch** and the second is called **Python**. You will be able to complete exciting projects in each of the languages, with plenty of help to guide you as you learn to **program**.

It is very important to check with an adult before downloading anything onto your computer. This helps to keep you safe on the internet, and will also keep your computer healthy!

How to use the tutorials

Learning to code is all about practising and experimenting. Follow each of the tutorials carefully, and make sure you read the instructions as well as looking at the picture guides.

Most importantly, once you have finished a tutorial, play around with your code. Try changing and adding extra bits, and don't worry if you break your code! All the best **programmers** in the world make mistakes, but fixing those mistakes (called **debugging**) is the best way to learn.

Scratch Programming language created for children that uses blocks of code which can be connected together to make programs

Python Programming language based on typing text which is designed to be simple to learn and use

Program Design and write code

There's even a famous quote about coding and making mistakes, by Mark Zuckerberg – the man who created Facebook:

Programmer Person who designs and writes code

Debugging Testing code to find and fix mistakes

"Move fast and break things. Unless you are breaking stuff, you are not moving fast enough."

MARC SCOTT

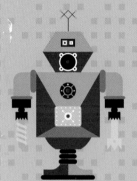

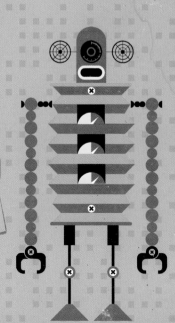

A Beginner's Guide to Coding

Illustrated by MICK MARSTON

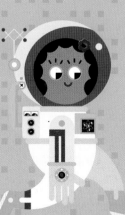

To James, the best code reviewer
a father could have.

First published 2016 by Bloomsbury Publishing Plc
50 Bedford Square, London, WC1B 3DP

www.bloomsbury.com

Bloomsbury is a registered trademark of Bloomsbury Publishing Plc

Text copyright © 2016 Marc Scott
Illustration copyright © 2016 Mick Marston

The rights of Marc Scott and Mick Marston to be identified as the author and
illustrator of this work respectively have been asserted by them in accordance with
the Copyrights, Designs and Patents Act 1988.

ISBN: 978-1-4729-2864-1

A CIP catalogue for this book is available from the British Library.

All Internet addresses given in this book were correct at the time of going to
press. The author and publishers regret any inconvenience caused if
addresses have changed or if websites have ceased to exist, but can
accept no responsibility for any such changes.

Printed in Italy by L.E.G.O Spa

1 3 5 7 9 10 8 6 4 2

Scratch is developed by the Lifelong Kindergarten Group at the MIT Media Lab.
See http://scratch.mit.edu." The SCRATCH name and loges
are trade marks owned by the Scratch Team.
For terms of use see: https://scratch.mit.edu/terms_of_use/

What is coding?

What are computers?

Computers are all around us. There are probably lots of computers in your house; you might not realise how many! Do you or your family have a laptop? Of course, that is a computer. But what about a mobile phone? Did you know that a mobile is a computer too? There's even a computer in your television, your microwave and your car. Sometimes we use computers that are hundreds, or even thousands, of miles away. When you use the Internet, the computer (called a server) that stores the web page you are looking at could be in a completely different country to you.

Computers are machines that can work out the answers to very easy maths problems. For instance, computers can add and subtract numbers, or they can tell whether two numbers are the same or not. They can do maths very quickly. If you tried to count to a million, it would probably take you over a week. A computer can count to a million in less than a second.

Being able to do maths quickly is impressive but the thing that makes computers really special is that they can follow instructions. These instructions are called **programs**. Computers can follow these instructions and do extremely clever things, like moving monsters around the screen in a computer game, or flying a real aeroplane to take you on holiday.

Without programs, a computer is completely useless. What actually makes computers so special is the programs that are written for them.

Programs
Collections of
instructions that a
computer follows
to perform
a task

What is coding?

When a programmer writes a computer program, they can't use any of the languages that people normally use to speak to each other. For instance, you can't simply say to a computer "count to one thousand". Instead, you have to use a special language called a programming language. There are hundreds of different languages that you can write programs in. If we wanted a computer to count to one thousand in Scratch, a programming language you will soon be learning, we would write:

Once you have finished writing a computer program it needs to be translated into 1s and 0s. This is called **compiling** or **interpreting**, and allows the computer to read the instructions. It doesn't matter which programming language you use, it always ends up being translated into 1s and 0s by the computer.

Compiling
Converting a program into a language that a computer can run

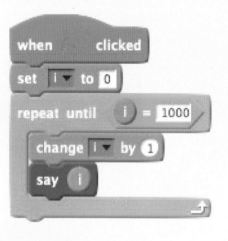

Interpreting
When a program is run by a computer, one line at a time

In Python, a language which you will learn later on in this book, we might instead write:

```python
for i in range(1001):
    print(i)
```

In another language called JavaScript we would write:

```javascript
for(i=0; i<1001; i++){
console.log(i)
};
```

The words and symbols used in programming languages are called **code**. So we often call writing computer programs **coding**.

Code
Instructions written in a programming language that a computer can follow

Coding
Writing code for a computer

What is syntax?

Syntax is the rules of a language. Look at these two sentences:

"I am an awesome coder."

"coder am an I awesome."

The first sentence makes sense, because it follows the syntax (or rules) of the English language. The second sentence doesn't follow the rules and doesn't make sense. You could probably work out what the sentence means, even though the words are in the wrong order, because you are an intelligent person. But computers aren't intelligent in the same way as you! They can't work out what you mean when you write code that isn't correct.

If you don't follow the rules of the programming language, the computer will not try to compile or interpret the instructions; instead it will just tell you that you've made a mistake. This is called a **syntax error**.

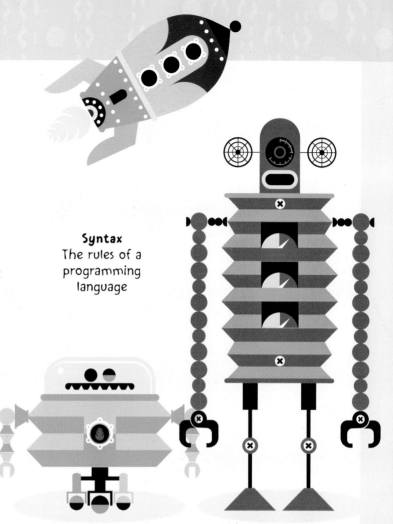

Syntax
The rules of a programming language

Syntax error
Mistake in a computer program caused by not following the rules of the programming language

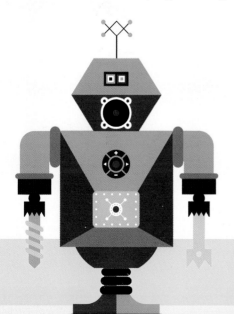

Why is coding important?

There are computers everywhere and they are doing many important jobs every day. We use computers to learn, to work, to play, to talk, to travel... and every time we use a computer, it works by running code that was written by a programmer. Without coders, computers wouldn't work and the world would be a very different place!

Scratch is a programming language that was designed to teach coding. You'll get the hang of it in no time, and then you can use it to create games, interactive stories and animations.

Before you start using Scratch, you're going to need to create an account, and if you are under 13 years old, you will need to talk to an adult and use their email address.

Setting up a Scratch account

1. Open up a web browser on your computer.
2. You need to go to *www.scratch.mit.edu*
3. You should see a | Join Scratch | button that you can click on.
4. Next you will need to choose a username and a password. Make sure you do not use your real name. Click | Next | when you are done.

Names on the Internet

The Internet is a great place to meet and talk to new people, but you don't always know who you are talking to, and whether you can trust them. You should always pick usernames that are different to your real name. Choose a favourite game or cartoon character, or even a pet's name.

Passwords

Passwords make sure nobody can use your account and pretend to be you. You should choose a password that nobody would be able to guess. It is a good idea to use a **passphrase** like:

`ILoveEatingHats`

or

`MyFishNeverSleeps`

Passphrase Group of words that is easy to remember but hard for someone else to guess

Join Scratch

Your responses to these questions will be kept private.
Why do we ask for this info ❓

Birth Month and Year   January ⬍   2008 ⬍

Gender   ◉ Male   ◯ Female   ◯ _____

Country   United Kingdom ⬍

5. Now you need to add in your age, gender and location before clicking on [Next].

Join Scratch   ✕

Enter your parent's or guardian's email address and we will send them an email to confirm this account.

Parent's or guardian's email address   my-parent@email.com

Confirm email address   my-parent@email.com

① ② ③ **4** ✉   [Next]

6. For the next part you will need a helpful adult. Ask them to fill in their email address in the spaces provided. They can check their email later to confirm their address.

Join Scratch   ✕

Welcome to Scratch, **awesome-coder-321**!

You're now logged in! You can start exploring and creating projects.

If you want to share and comment, simply click the link in the email we sent you at ▬▬▬▬▬▬▬▬▬

Wrong email? Change your email address in Account Settings.

Having problems? Please give us feedback

① ② ③ ④ ✉   [OK Lets Go!]

7. If you see a screen like this one, then it means you have been registered with the Scratch website, and you're ready to start coding!

8. Click on the [OK Lets Go!] button, to begin exploring Scratch.

The **Toolbar** is where you can choose options like saving your project or creating a new one.

Getting around

1. To understand the projects in this book, you are going to need to know a little bit about the **Scratch Graphical User Interface** (GUI).

2. On the main page, click on Create

3. You should see a screen like the one on the next page.

Graphical User Interface
The (GUI) Screen lets you click buttons, or choose items from a menu, usually using your mouse, trackpad or touch screen

The **Stage** is where you can see your project running.

The **Sprites Pane** is where you can keep all the images you will use in the project.

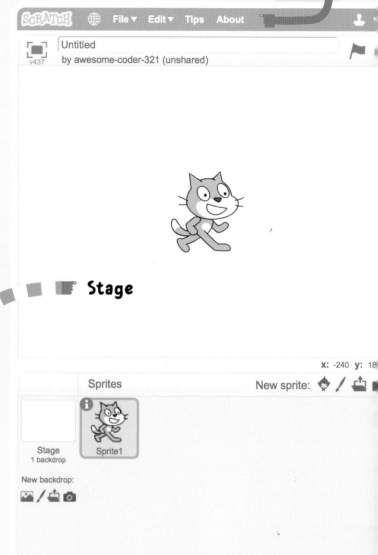

Toolbar

Stage

Sprites Pane

The **Script Area** is where you will place all your code for the project.

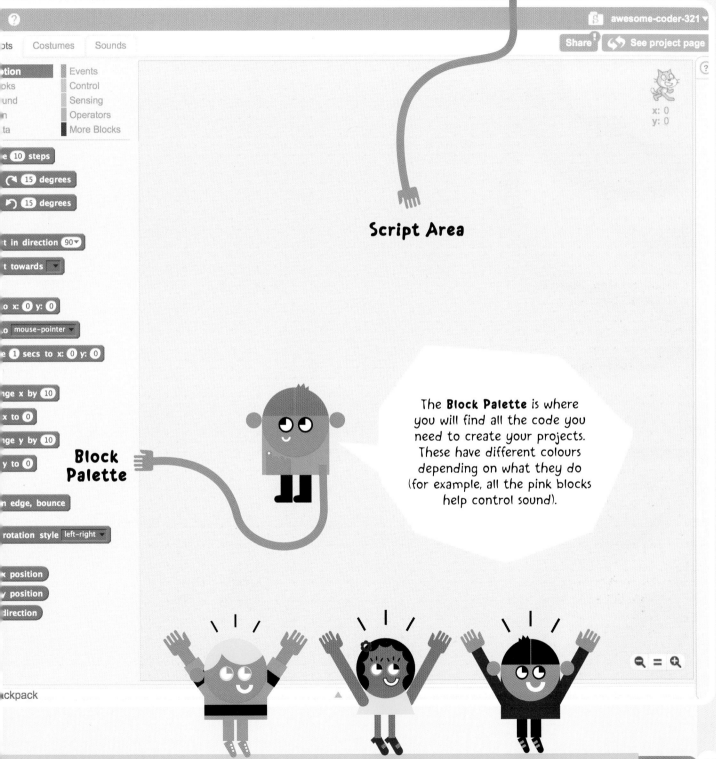

The **Block Palette** is where you will find all the code you need to create your projects. These have different colours depending on what they do (for example, all the pink blocks help control sound).

Script Area

Block Palette

Costumes   Sounds

Events
Control
Sensing
Operators
More Blocks

tion
oks
und
n
ta

10 steps
15 degrees
15 degrees
t in direction 90▾
t towards ▾
o x: 0 y: 0
o mouse-pointer ▾
e 1 secs to x: 0 y: 0
nge x by 10
x to 0
nge y by 10
y to 0
n edge, bounce
rotation style left-right ▾
x position
y position
direction

x: 0
y: 0

awesome-coder-321 ▾
Share   See project page

ckpack

Now you know a little bit about SCRATCH let's start on the next chapter, and code your first project!

Talk to the animals

Now it's time to get started - let's see if you can code a game that lets the player talk to an animal character.

Sprites
Images used in computer games

Sprites

1. Programmers call the pictures used in computer programs 'sprites'.

2. In the Sprites Pane, you will see a cat sprite.

3. Delete this sprite by right-clicking on it and then clicking on 'delete'.

4. Click on the 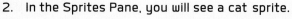 in the Sprites Pane to see all the amazing sprites you can use in Scratch.

5. Here is the starfish, but you can choose any sprite you like – how about a dragon, a dinosaur, or a baby elephant?

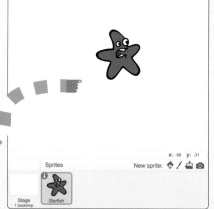

Talking

1. Now we will make the sprite talk using something called a custom block.

2. Click on the **More Blocks** menu in the Block Palette (make sure you are in the Scripts tab).

3. Now click on **Make a Block** .

New Block

sayHello

▶ Options

OK   Cancel

4. We can call the new block 'sayHello', by typing this into the purple box.

5. Then click on **OK** .

6. Let's add some code to our custom block!

7. Click on the **Looks** menu.

8. We want to drag the **say Hello! for 2 secs** from the Block Palette and connect it to the **define sayHello** that we just made (a white line will appear between the two blocks, drag the new block over this and they will join together, like a jigsaw!)

Custom block
A Scratch block that does a specific task

9. Now, if you click on the script you have just made, the sprite should say "Hello!"

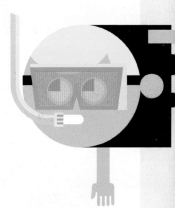

Script
Small section of code, which can be as short as a few lines or as long as hundreds of lines. In Scratch, a script is a collection of blocks that you have joined together.

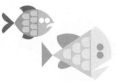

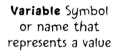

Variable Symbol or name that represents a value

Asking questions

1. Our sprite is talking to us, but wouldn't it be cool if we could talk back to it?

2. Make a new custom block just like you did before, but call it askName .

3. Click on the **Sensing** menu and drag the block `ask What's your name? and wait` onto your new custom block.

4. Test your new block by clicking on it.

5. Type your name into the box at the bottom and press 'enter' on your keyboard.

6. Although you gave the program your name, you didn't tell the program to remember it. For the program to remember your name, we can use a **variable**. Variables allow programs to store bits of data like names or numbers.

7. In the **Data** menu click on `Make a Variable` .

8. We will call the variable `playerName` .

New Variable

Variable name: playerName

● For all sprites   ○ For this sprite only

OK   Cancel

9. Now there will be some new blocks to choose from in the Block Palette. We want the `set playerName ▼ to 0` block. Drag it to the bottom of your new custom block, so it looks like this:

10. We need to change the value of 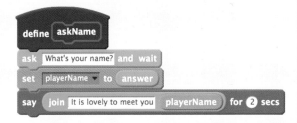 playerName because at the moment it is set to 'O', which is not your name!

11. Click on the Sensing menu and drag the answer block into the set playerName ▼ to 0 , so it replaces the O.

define askName

ask What's your name? and wait
set playerName ▼ to answer

12. Your name has now been saved by the program, and the sprite can use your name.

13. Click on Looks and then drag the say Hello! for 2 secs block onto the bottom of your custom block.

14. Click on Operators , and drag the join hello world block into your custom block, so that it replaces the word 'Hello'.

define askName

ask What's your name? and wait
set playerName ▼ to answer
say join hello world for 2 secs

15. Change the first part of the block so that it says "It's lovely to meet you ". Make sure you leave an extra space at the end of the sentence, so that the last word won't merge with the start of your name.

16. Now click on Data and drag the variable playerName into the second part of the join block.

define askName

ask What's your name? and wait
set playerName ▼ to answer
say join It is lovely to meet you playerName for 2 secs

17. Left-click on your finished custom block to see it working... your sprite should ask your name, and when you reply, it should say "It is lovely to meet you [name]". What a polite sprite!

Hi!   Hello!

Running it all together

1. Now that we have two custom blocks we can join them so that they run, one after the other, without having to click on them every time.

2. From **Events** drag the `when clicked` block onto the Script Area.

3. From **More Blocks** you can now attach your two custom blocks to the bottom of it.

4. Now click the 🚩 at the top of the stage to see your program working.

5. Well done: you've created your first computer program! You're well on your way to being an awesome coder.

Talking back

1. We can make the sprite say different things when it is given different answers.

2. Create a new custom block and call it `askAge`.

3. Now use the `ask What's your name? and wait` block, but change it so that it asks, "How old are you?"

4. Next we need a new variable called `playerAge`. As we did before, click on `Make a Variable` in **Data** and type in "playerAge". Then add the `set playerAge to 0` block to your script. If you get mixed up with the different variable names, you can choose the correct one by clicking on the little black arrow. Next drag `answer` from **Sensing** into the block. It should look like this when you are ready:

5. We are now going to make the sprite say different things, depending on the player's age. To do this we need this block:

 You can find it in the **Control** menu of the Block Palette. Drag it to the bottom of your custom block.

6. In the **Operators** section of the Block Palette find the `[ ] = [ ]` and place it into the block:

7. Think of an age you want your sprite to be. We can add this into the `[ ] = [ ]` with the `playerAge`, as well as using a `say Hello! for 2 secs` block. See if you can use these blocks to make this finished script:

8. We can finish this off using another block:

Drag it to the bottom of your custom block, so it sits inside the 'else' you used before.

9. We can use the `[ ] > [ ]` block to see if the `playerAge` is greater than the age you chose, and to make the sprite say something. If the age is not equal to or not greater than the number you chose,

then it must be less than, and we can add a different response.

10. Finish off by adding your **askAge** block (from **More Blocks**) to the bottom of the `when clicked` block:

11. Run your program by clicking on the ⚑ and have a short conversation with your animal sprite!

Can you take a challenge?

- Try and create a new custom block to ask another question, for example:

    What's your favourite food?

- You could make your sprite give different responses depending on the player's answer.

- See if you can add in a second sprite that could join in the conversation.

17

Painting pictures in SCRATCH

Can you guess how this picture was made?

It was created using a computer and some clever mathematics! It is called a **fractal** and if you look online you will find lots of examples of them. Fractals are amazing pictures created using repeating patterns.

Fractal
Never-ending and repeating pattern

In this project you are going to use Scratch to create some pictures of your own.

Basic drawing

1. First, you should create a new Scratch project and delete the cat sprite, like you did in the last project.

2. Next, choose a new sprite from the library. This time, choose an arrow, as it makes it easy to see which way it is pointing.

3. Now you need to make a new custom block (remember, we can find this in **More Blocks**). Call it **drawLine** .

4. In the Block Palette click on **Pen** .

5. Select the **pen down** block from the Block Palette and drag it onto the Script Area, then add it to the bottom of the custom block.

6. We need to move the sprite so that we can make it draw a line. From **Motion** drag a **move 10 steps** block onto the Script Area and connect it to the bottom of the **pen down** . Change the 10 to 100. Then add a **pen up** to the end.

7. Your block should look like this:

8. Now, when you click on the custom block, you should see the arrow move and leave a line behind it.

9. We need to clear the Stage now and put the arrow back to the middle. Create a new custom block and call it **reset** .

10. To the bottom of the block, add **go to x: 0 y: 0** from the **Motion** section of the Block Palette, and then **clear** from the **Pen** palette. When you click on your new reset block, it should clear the screen and send the arrow back to the middle of the Stage.

11. Your Script Area should now look like this:

12. Each time you click on the **define reset** block, the line will vanish and the arrow will go back to the middle of the Stage.

Every time you click on the **define drawLine** block, a new line will be drawn.

Drawing shapes

1. Lines on their own aren't very exciting, but they can be used to make lots of other shapes, if we use an **algorithm**.

Algorithm Set of simple steps to solve a problem. The problem could be crossing a road safely, in which case the algorithm would look like this:

1. Look left.

2. Look right.

3. Look left again.

4. If there are no cars coming.

5. Cross the road.

2. Create a new custom block called **drawShape** .

3. To draw a square we need to draw a line 4 times, and turn ninety degrees after each line has been drawn. Try and build this script:

```
define drawShape
drawLine
turn ↻ 90 degrees
drawLine
turn ↻ 90 degrees
drawLine
turn ↻ 90 degrees
drawLine
turn ↻ 90 degrees
```

4. Click on the block and you should see a square has been draw on the stage.

5. If we want to draw a different shape, like an octagon, it would take a lot of clicking and dragging to build up our script.

6. We can use a loop to make our job a little easier. Click on **Control** in the Block Palette and find the

 block.

7. Anything placed inside this block will happen 10 times. That's too much for us, so change the 10 to a 4. Then you need to completely change your **drawShape** custom block so that it looks like this:

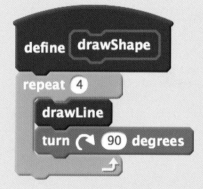

```
define drawShape
repeat 4
  drawLine
  turn ↻ 90 degrees
```

8. Click your block and your square will be drawn.

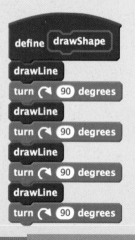

More complicated shapes

Wouldn't it be better if we could draw more than just a square with the **drawShape** custom block? Well with **input** we can!

Input
Data that is received by a computer program

1. Hold down the 'shift' key on your keyboard and click on your **drawShape** block and a menu will pop up.

2. Choose 'edit':

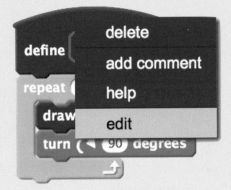

3. Click on the little arrow next to the word 'Options' and a menu will appear. Choose 'Add number input':

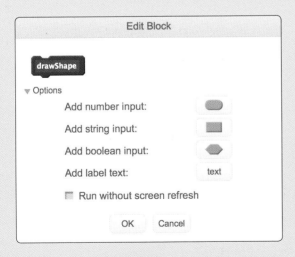

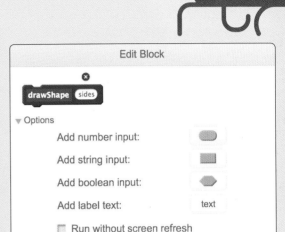

4. Type in the word 'sides' in the space next to drawShape.

5. Your custom block will now look like this:

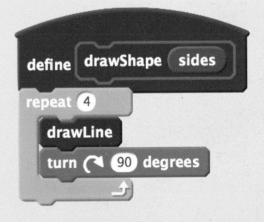

6. You can also use the **sides** variable in the rest of the script. Drag **sides** so that it replaces the number 4.

21

7. Now we need to change the number of degrees that the sprite turns. We turned by 90 degrees for a square, because each corner in a square has a 90 degree angle. We can work this out: there are 360 degrees in a whole turn. When we divide 360 by 4 (because there are 4 corners, and so 4 angles, in a square), we get 90. This time we are going to use a (/) from **Operators** to work out the degrees our sprite must turn to draw a different shape.

8. Alter your custom block so it looks like this:

```
define drawShape sides

repeat sides
    drawLine
    turn ↻ 360 / sides degrees
```

9. Clicking on your block won't work now, because you need to tell it how many sides to draw. From **More Blocks** drag **drawShape 1** into the Script Area.

10. Change the 1 to a 6 and then click **drawShape 6**. See what happens and then try some other numbers.

Even more complicated shapes

How about something a little more complicated? Let's draw a flower. You're not going to get as much help finding the blocks in this one, as you should be turning into an expert by now!

1. First, we'll need to draw a petal. Use what you have learned to create the custom block shown here:

```
define petal size

pen down
repeat 2
    repeat 90
        move size steps
        turn ↻ 1 degrees
    turn ↻ 90 degrees
```

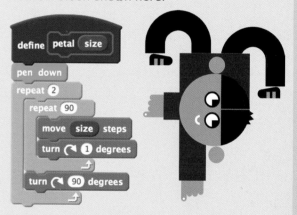

2. Now grab the **petal 1** block from **More Blocks** and place it in the Script Area. You can change the number to set the size of the petal and then click it to draw. Just click on:

define reset

if you want to clear the screen.

3. Now you have a petal, you can draw a flower! Have a go at creating this custom block. You'll need to give it two 'Add number input' blocks by clicking 'Add number input' twice.

```
define flower petals size
repeat petals
    petal size
    turn ↻ 360 / petals degrees
```

4. Grab the `flower 1 1` block and place it somewhere in the Script Area. If you change the first number it will increase the number of petals. The second number will increase the size of the petals. Click on it to draw the flower.

Super flowers

By using more repeat loops and changing the colour of the pen, we can come up with some really awesome patterns. See if you can build this block:

```
when      clicked
go to x: 0 y: 0
clear
set pen color to 0
set petals ▾ to 4
repeat 12
    set size ▾ to 2
    repeat 12
        flower petals size
        change size ▾ by -0.1
        change pen color by 7
    change petals ▾ by 0.5
```

Experimenting with different values for the variables will give you some cool patterns. Before you click on the 🏳 put Scratch into turbo mode to speed things up a little. Hold down the 'shift' key on your keyboard and click the 🏳 to start turbo mode.

A note on coordinates in Scratch

The position of a sprite on the Stage is represented in Scratch with two numbers, called x and y.

The x number sets the side to side position of the sprite.

The y number sets the up and down position of the sprite.

x:0 y:0 is the middle of the screen.

If we increase the value of x, then the sprite moves right.

If we decrease the value of x, then the sprite moves left.

If we increase the value of y, then the sprite moves up.

If we decrease the value of y, then the sprite moves down.

Read on to use coordinates in a space game!

The clones attack

Now that you know your way around Scratch, it's time to make our first game! We are going to start with a game where the player controls a spaceship and has to avoid some flying robots.

Controlling a spaceship

1. Create a new Scratch project.

2. Delete the cat sprite and then use the icon to choose a new backdrop for the Stage. A space backdrop would look good for this game.

3. Next, you need to choose a new sprite: let's use the spaceship sprite.

4. Let's begin by making sure that when the game starts, the spaceship is the correct size, is in the correct place, and is facing in the correct direction. To do this, make a block like the next graphic.

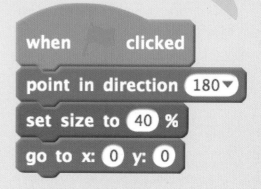

5. Now comes the fun part... let's make the spaceship move! To do this we will need a

forever loop, which will run as long as the game is being played. A 'forever' block is really useful for detecting things that are happening in a game, like key presses or sprites hitting each other.

6. Drag a forever loop from **Control** in the Block Palette, onto the bottom of your script. We want to tell our program to react when a key is pressed. So inside the loop place an

if ⬡ then block, and then from **Sensing** drag in the

`key space ▼ pressed?` block.

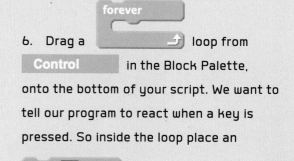

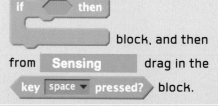

```
when [] clicked
point in direction 180▾
set size to 40 %
go to x: 0 y: 0
forever
    if < key space ▾ pressed? > then

```

7. Which key should we choose and what will happen when it's pressed? Let's start with the 'up' arrow key. We want the y position of the spaceship to increase by ten every time the 'up' arrow is pressed.

```
if < key up arrow ▾ pressed? > then
    change y by 10
```

8. By shift-clicking on this block we can choose 'duplicate' from the menu, to save us getting all the blocks from the palette again.

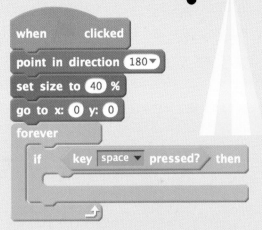

```
when [] clicked
point in direction 180▾
set size to 40 %
go to x: 0 y: 0
forever
    if  key up arrow  pressed?  then
    ┌─────────────────────┐
    │ duplicate           │
    │ delete              │
    │ add comment         │
    │ help                │
    └─────────────────────┘
```

9. Duplicate it 3 times, and then change the keys pressed and the directions: drag the `change x by 10` block to replace the `change y by 10` blocks in the last two duplications. It should end up looking like this:

```
when [] clicked
point in direction 180▾
set size to 40 %
go to x: 0 y: 0
forever
    if < key up arrow ▾ pressed? > then
        change y by 10
    if < key down arrow ▾ pressed? > then
        change y by -10
    if < key right arrow ▾ pressed? > then
        change x by 10
    if < key left arrow ▾ pressed? > then
        change x by -10
```

10. You can now press the 🏳 and have a go at controlling the spaceship!

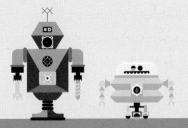

25

Endless robots

Now we have our spaceship working, let's make some robots to throw at it.

1. Grab the robot sprite from the Sprites Pane.

2. It's facing the wrong way to start with, so we need to change the robot's costume to flip it around. Click on the 'Costumes' tab at the top of the screen.

3. Now find the [DI] button in the top left of the screen and click it to flip the robot around.

4. Click back onto the 'Scripts' tab when you are done.

5. Just like we did with the spaceship, we need to change the robot's size and position:

   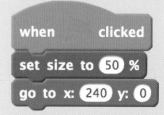

6. Now we want to send lots of robots flying at the spaceship. It would take us a long time to create hundreds of sprites so instead we are going to use **clones** of the robot.

Clones
Copies of a sprite and all its scripts

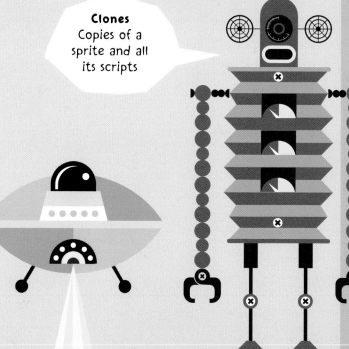

7. First we want to use a 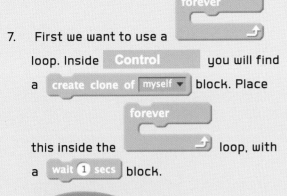 loop. Inside **Control** you will find a `create clone of myself ▼` block. Place this inside the `forever` loop, with a `wait 1 secs` block.

```
when ⚑ clicked
set size to 50 %
go to x: 240 y: 0
forever
    create clone of myself ▼
    wait 1 secs
```

8. Nothing will happen yet, because all the clones are created on top of the original robot. We need to make them move when they are created. We can do this by making a new script like this one:

```
when I start as a clone
forever
    move -5 steps
```

9. Now click the ⚑ to see your robot clones flying across the screen!

Randomness

We can now do three things to make the game more interesting:

1. Make the game end if the robot touches the spaceship.

2. Make the robots appear at random.

3. Make sure the robots disappear when they leave the screen.

Let's put these finishing touches to the game you have created:

1. To end the game when the robot touches the spaceship we can use a script like this:

```
if touching Spaceship ▼ ? then
    stop all ▼
```

2. The `stop all ▼` block makes all the running scripts end.

3. Place this into the clone's forever loop:

```
when I start as a clone
forever
    move -5 steps
    if touching Spaceship ▼ ? then
        stop all ▼
```

4. Now click the 🏳 and see what happens when a robot hits the spaceship.

5. Let's make the robot's starting position less easy to guess. In **Operators** you will find a `pick random 1 to 10` block. This block will pick random numbers, which we can use to change the position of the clones.

6. Use the `pick random 1 to 10` block and add it so that you have made the script below:

```
when I start as a clone
go to x: 240 y: pick random -150 to 150
forever
    move -5 steps
    if   touching Spaceship ? then
        stop all
```

7. Click the 🏳 to see if your scripts are working. The robots should be appearing at random positions on the screen. If they're not doing this, go back and check all your blocks to see if you can spot the problem.

8. Our last step is to destroy the clones when they reach the other side of the screen.

9. To do this we need to know if their x position is less than about -230. This is

because the Scratch stage goes from +240 (on the right) to -240 (on the left). So if the robot is at -230 it must be about to hit the left-hand edge of the stage. The `⬚ < ⬚` can be found in **Operators**.

10. Use some extra blocks from **Control** as well as the `⬚ < ⬚` block, and finish off the clone script so that it looks like this:

```
when I start as a clone
go to x: 240 y: pick random -150 to 150
forever
    move -5 steps
    if   touching Spaceship ? then
        stop all

    if   x position < -230 then
        delete this clone
```

11. One last thing... the original robot is always visible at the edge of the screen, but it is just sitting there. We can solve this by hiding the sprite but showing the clones. You can find **hide** and **show** in **Looks**. Add these into the scripts you have already built:

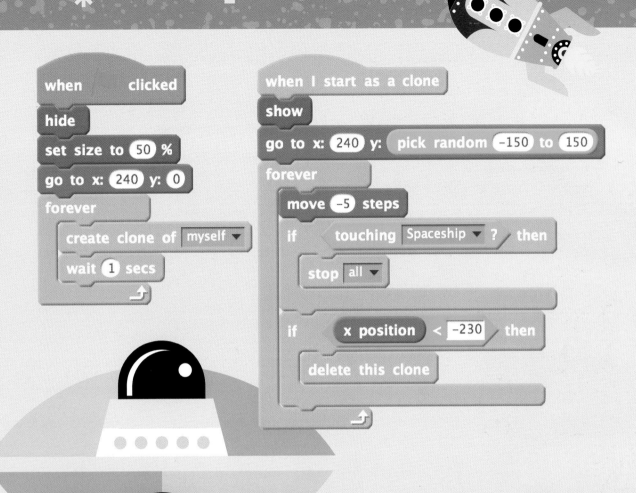

```
when    clicked
hide
set size to 50 %
go to x: 240 y: 0
forever
    create clone of myself ▼
    wait 1 secs
```

```
when I start as a clone
show
go to x: 240 y: pick random -150 to 150
forever
    move -5 steps
    if    touching Spaceship ▼ ?    then
        stop all ▼

    if    x position < -230    then
        delete this clone
```

Can you take a challenge?

- The next part is up to you — be creative and don't be afraid of breaking things!

- You could make the game a little harder by using a `pick random 1 to 10` block to set the speed of the robot clones, so that some are very fast and some are very slow.

- At the moment the robots always have a speed of -5. You could make a new variable called `speed` to replace the -5 and then use the `change speed ▾ by 1` block to change how fast the robot goes.

- Perhaps you could make the spaceship fire a missile (using clones again), which could destroy the robots.

- Here is an example of a trickier version of the robot script, in case you are stuck for ideas:

```
when       clicked
set  speed ▾ to -5
set  level ▾ to 1
set  delay ▾ to 2
set  score ▾ to 0
hide
forever
    create clone of myself ▾
    wait delay secs
    if      score = 10  then
        set  score ▾ to 0
        change delay ▾ by -0.1
        change level ▾ by 1
        change speed ▾ by -2
```

```
when I start as a clone
show
go to x: 240 y: pick random -150 to 150
forever
    move speed steps
    if      touching Spaceship ▾ ?  then
        stop all ▾

    if      x position < -230  then
    change score ▾ by 1
    delete this clone
```

Dance hero

In this chapter you're going to make your very own dance game, using images of yourself as the dancer!

Getting the images

1. Ask an adult to help you with this bit. You need to use a digital camera, a phone, a tablet or even your webcam to take photos of yourself. Make sure you are in a brightly lit room, and try to take pictures of yourself against a plain coloured wall or door.

2. You will need five photos: one standing normally and four in a variety of dancing positions.

3. Transfer the photos to your computer and then rename each of them so that they are called 'Start,' 'Right,' 'Left,' 'Up' and 'Down'. If you don't have access to a camera, or don't want to upload your images, you can use any of the dance sprites that are already available in Scratch.

Adding the images to Scratch

1. Start a new Scratch project and delete the cat sprite. In the Sprites Pane click on the icon and choose the photo you called 'Start' from your computer.

2. Click on the 'Costumes' tab and you should see the image.

3. We need to remove the background from the photo. Use the icon to select the 'Erase' tool, and then carefully remove the background from the picture.

4. If you make a mistake you can undo the last action using the icon and you can zoom in and out using the controls. You should finish with an image that looks something like this:

New costume:

1

Start
89x273

2

Right
89x275

3

Left
78x285

4

Up
91x343

5 ✕

Down
91x210

5. Now, staying in the 'Costumes' tab, click on the 📤 to upload a second costume. Choose the 'Right' photo next.

6. Again, remove the background, and then upload the next costume. Keep going until you have uploaded all the photos, and all the costumes are listed on the left.

Adding some tunes

1. You can use music from the 'Sounds' library, record some from your computer's microphone or upload some music from your computer.

2. Click on the 'Sounds' tab.

3. Now choose one of the 🔊 🎤 📤 icons, and either pick a music loop, record some music or upload a music file from your computer.

4. We're going to need 5 pieces of music for this project.

New sound:

🔊 🎤 📤

1

My Music
03:10.01

2

dance space
00:04.00

3

dance slow mo
00:20.21

4

techno2
00:14.83

5 ✕

techno
00:07.96

Making the music play

1. We're going to want to change the track that's being played. So we need to make a variable which will store the track numbers.

2. Click on the 'Scripts' tab and then click on **Data** .

3. Click on **Make a Variable** and call the variable **Track** .

4. Now we'll build our script to start the music playing. Have a go at building the script below. You can find the

   play sound My Music in the **Sound** menu.

5. Click on the  and make sure that the music plays. Make sure to check that your volume is turned up, if you can't hear anything.

Setting the stage

1. We want a disco style backdrop for our game!

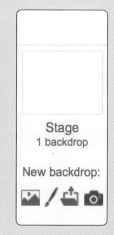

2. Over in the 'Stage' section, choose a new backdrop by clicking on the icon.

3. Choose any one of the 'Music and Dance' backdrops that you like.

4. Position your dancer within the Stage, and use the icons to resize the sprite if you need to.

Making the sprite dance

Start

1. Make sure you have clicked back on to your 'Start' sprite.

2. Now modify the 'Start' script to set the starting costume.

3. You'll work out the next part in no time!

```
when    clicked
switch costume to Start ▼
set  Track ▼ to 1
forever
    play sound  Track  until done
```

We need four small scripts to make the sprite change costume, when the player presses the arrow keys.

4. Add the scripts shown below:

```
when down arrow ▼ key pressed
switch costume to Down ▼
```
```
when right arrow ▼ key pressed
switch costume to Right ▼
```
```
when up arrow ▼ key pressed
switch costume to Up ▼
```
```
when left arrow ▼ key pressed
switch costume to Left ▼
```

5. All the scripts you've made for your dancer so far should look like this:

```
when    clicked
switch costume to Start ▼
set  Track ▼ to 1
forever
    play sound  Track  until done
```

```
when down arrow ▼ key pressed
switch costume to Down ▼
```
```
when left arrow ▼ key pressed
switch costume to Left ▼
```
```
when right arrow ▼ key pressed
switch costume to Right ▼
```
```
when up arrow ▼ key pressed
switch costume to Up ▼
```

6. Click on the ⚑ and then use the arrow keys to make your sprite dance to the music.

Making the game

Now we have a dancing sprite, we can start to make the game. First we'll need an arrow sprite:

1. Click on the 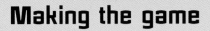 icon in the 'Sprites' panel.

2. Find the ➡ sprite.

3. Now we are going to add a few scripts to the arrow sprite.

4. In our game, the player will have 5 lives and the speed of the game will start at 1 and then increase. Your computer will need a few variables in your program to store that data.

```
when      clicked
set  lives ▾  to 5
set  speed ▾  to 1
```

5. First we need to set the starting position of the sprite and then hide it:

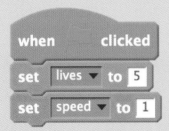

```
when      clicked
set  lives ▾  to 5
set  speed ▾  to 1
go to x: -200  y: -125
hide
```

6. Next we need to randomly change the arrow's costume, and make a clone of it.

```
when      clicked
set  lives ▾  to 5
set  speed ▾  to 1
go to x: -200  y: -125
hide
forever
    switch costume to  pick random 1 to 4
    create clone of  myself ▾
    wait  speed  secs
```

7. When the clone is created, we need it to become visible and then start to move across the screen.

```
when I start as a clone
show
forever
    move  3 / speed  steps
```

8. Click on the 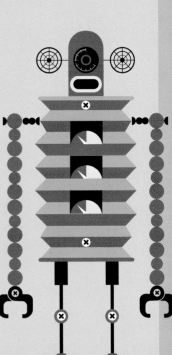 and make sure that the arrows are moving across the screen.

9. Let's make the arrows change colour when they get below the dancer. We can make the arrows change their colour effect when their
`x position` is between -30 and 30.

```
when I start as a clone
show
forever
    move 3 / speed steps
    if      x position > -30  and   x position < 30  then
        change color ▼ effect by 15
```

10. Click on the 🚩 and make sure that the arrows change colour.

11. Now for the player's controls. We want the player to have to press the correct key on their keyboard when the arrow changes colour – their timing will have to be pretty good! First create this script, which detects the key being pressed, and checks whether the arrow's costume is the one pointing towards the right.

```
if     key right arrow ▼ pressed?  and   costume # = 1  then
    delete this clone
```

12. We can copy this script another three times, by shift-clicking on it and choosing 'duplicate'.

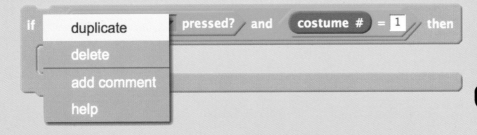

```
if  | duplicate        | pressed?  and   costume # = 1  then
    | delete           |
    | add comment      |
    | help             |
```

13. Now join the scripts together and change the keys and costume values for all three duplicates, so that it looks like this:

```
if  key [right arrow ▾] pressed?  and  costume # = 1  then
  delete this clone

if  key [left arrow ▾] pressed?  and  costume # = 2  then
  delete this clone

if  key [down arrow ▾] pressed?  and  costume # = 3  then
  delete this clone

if  key [up arrow ▾] pressed?  and  costume # = 4  then
  delete this clone
```

14. We've finished building the key detection script now, so add it into the clone's script:

```
when I start as a clone
show
forever
  move (3 / speed) steps
  if  x position > -30  and  x position < 30  then
    change [color ▾] effect by 15
    if  key [right arrow ▾] pressed?  and  costume # = 1  then
      delete this clone
    if  key [left arrow ▾] pressed?  and  costume # = 2  then
      delete this clone
    if  key [down arrow ▾] pressed?  and  costume # = 3  then
      delete this clone
    if  key [up arrow ▾] pressed?  and  costume # = 4  then
      delete this clone
```

15. Click on the 🏁 and make sure that the arrows get deleted when you press the keys at the right time.

Making the game more difficult

It would be nice if the game became more difficult as it was played. We can use the timer from **Sensing** to do this.

1. On your arrow sprite, add in this script, which will start a timer and make the game trickier every minute that it is played:

2. Click on the 🏁 to see if the arrows get faster after a minute.

3. If a minute is too long to wait, you can change the `timer > 60` to something shorter like 15 seconds: `timer > 15`

```
when 🏁 clicked
reset timer
forever
  if  timer > 60  then
    reset timer
    change [speed ▾] by -0.2
```

Changing the music

Let's change the music when the game speeds up!

1. On the arrow sprite, grab a
   `broadcast message1 ▼` block from
   `Events`.

2. Now create a new message:
   `broadcast Change Track ▼` and place
   it in the script after the speed has
   been changed.

3. Now you need to click on your sprite.

4. To change the music track, add in this
   new script:

5. Click on the 🏴 and make sure that the
   music changes when the arrows speed up.

Game over

1. Finally, we want the game to end if the
   player makes too many mistakes.

2. Click back on the ⬅ and create this
   script to detect if a clone is touching
   the edge of the screen.

3. Now place this new script into the main loop of the clone so that the script looks like this:

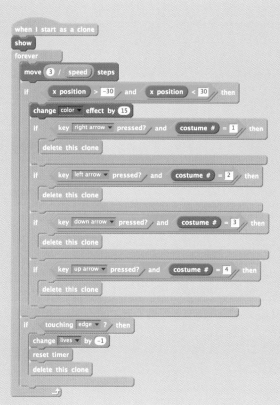

```
when I start as a clone
show
forever
    move ( 3 / speed ) steps
    if  ( x position > -30 ) and ( x position < 30 )  then
        change color effect by 15
        if  ( key right arrow pressed? ) and ( costume # = 1 )  then
            delete this clone

        if  ( key left arrow pressed? ) and ( costume # = 2 )  then
            delete this clone

        if  ( key down arrow pressed? ) and ( costume # = 3 )  then
            delete this clone

        if  ( key up arrow pressed? ) and ( costume # = 4 )  then
            delete this clone

    if  ( touching edge ? )  then
    change lives by -1
    reset timer
    delete this clone
```

4. Our final script will tell the player that the game is over. Let's add this to our sprite:

```
when [green flag] clicked
forever
    if  ( lives = 0 )  then
        say [You lost] for 2 secs
        stop all
```

5. Click on the and get your groove on with your dance hero game!

Can you take a challenge?
- See if you can make the backdrop change to a gameover screen when the player's lives reach 0
- keep track of the number of correct key presses the player makes, so that you can tell them their score at the end of the game.
- Try and adjust the speeds that you use and the track order, so that the player's key presses match the beat of the music
- You could add in another set of arrows, and have a second player in the game, using the 'w', 'a', 's', 'd' keys.

Are you ready for Python?

Python

Python is a programming language, just like Scratch, but instead of moving and joining blocks, you write your code using text.

Python was created by a man called Guido van Rossum. It is a little harder to use than Scratch, but it is a very powerful language. Well-known companies like Google and Apple use Python to write some of their **software**.

When you write code in Python it looks like this:

```
def sayHello():
    print('Hello')

sayHello()
```

You are going to learn how to use the version of Python which is called Python 3. Start off by asking an adult to help you install Python 3 on your computer by visiting **https://www.python.org/downloads**

There you should find a link to download and install Python 3.

Once you have installed Python you should find a new program called IDLE on your computer. You can write Python code with lots of different programs, but as a beginner, it is easiest to use IDLE.

Software
Programs or collections of programs that run on your computer. Your web browser is a type of software, as is IDLE, which you'll be using in this chapter.

A quick note on deleting
Once you have pressed 'enter', you can't delete the commands you have written.

Don't worry if you make a mistake - you can just type your code again correctly.

IDLE

1. Find IDLE and open it. Now you can start to learn how to code with Python! Depending on your computer, IDLE might look slightly different to the pictures in this book, but don't worry, it will not affect your code.

2. What you are now looking at is the Python **shell**:

```
Python 3.4.3 (default, Jun 10 2015, 19:56:14)
[GCC 4.2.1 Compatible Apple LLVM 6.1.0 (clang-602.0.53)] on darwin
Type "copyright", "credits" or "license()" for more information.
>>> |
```

> **Shell** Program that follows written instructions

3. The shell is a little like the Stage in Scratch, but it will only display text. It doesn't look as fun as Scratch, but it can do some cool things, as you'll soon find out! The shell is a place where you can write code that will be run straight away. It's a great place to test small lines of code to see what they do.

4. Unlike the Stage in Scratch, in Python we can type code straight into the shell.

5. Try typing these commands and see what happens. Press 'enter' on your keyboard after each one.

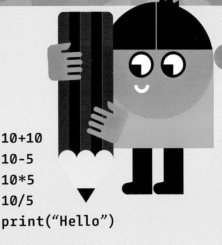

```
10+10
10-5
10*5
10/5
print("Hello")

print("Hello" * 100)
```

Syntax

Do you remember reading, in the first chapter, how important syntax is? Let's test that out.

1. Try typing the following command in the shell:

```
print("Hello)
```

2. You should get an error message telling you 'SyntaxError: EOL while scanning string literal'.

3. This just means you forgot to place a " after the word: 'Hello'.

4. Try typing the command again, with the " after the word.

Be prepared to make lots of mistakes and get lots of warnings like this. Remember, programmers learn by making mistakes and then trying to figure out what they did wrong. Even the best programmers in the world make silly mistakes like forgetting to put a " in their code.

Turtles all the way

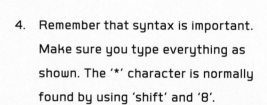

Some turtley awesome commands

1. Open IDLE.

2. We're going to play around with a part of Python called 'turtle'. This is a module used for drawing with Python.

Module

Code that has been written by other people, that you can use in your own programs. Programmers don't like re-writing code that already exists, so they use modules to help speed things up.

3. In the shell type the following command and press 'enter'. Don't worry if nothing happens.

```
from turtle import *
```

4. Remember that syntax is important. Make sure you type everything as shown. The '*' character is normally found by using 'shift' and '8'.

5. We're going to give our turtle a shape. Type this into the shell.

```
shape("turtle")
```

6. A new screen will appear, with a picture of a turtle in the middle. It is best to arrange your screens side by side, like this:

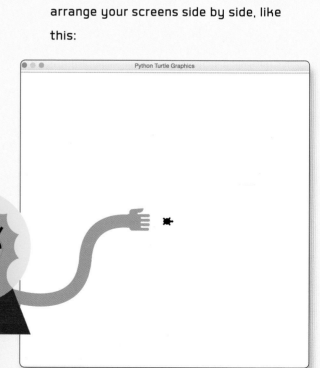

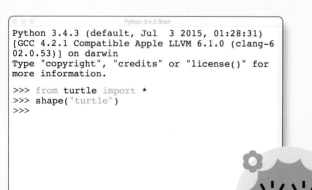

```
                    Python 3.4.3 Shell
Python 3.4.3 (default, Jul  3 2015, 01:28:31)
[GCC 4.2.1 Compatible Apple LLVM 6.1.0 (clang-6
02.0.53)] on darwin
Type "copyright", "credits" or "license()" for
more information.

>>> from turtle import *
>>> shape("turtle")
>>>
```

Python Turtle Graphics

7. Now let's move our turtle around. Type this into the shell:

```
fd(100)
rt(90)
fd(100)
```

You might have realised that 'fd' means forward and 'rt' means right. We can also use 'bk' for backward and 'lt' for left. If we type 'lt (90)' it means we're turning our turtle by 90 degrees:

```
bk(100)
lt(90)
```

8. Now try moving the turtle around the screen. Change the numbers in the brackets to turn and move it by different values.

9. Try to draw some different shapes with the turtle. If you lose it you can always bring it home by typing:

```
home()
```

Controlling the turtle's pen

1. Let's bring our turtle home and then clear the screen of our drawings so far.

```
home()
clear()
```

You can do this anytime you want to start a fresh drawing.

2. We can also control the colour and width of the pen that our turtle uses to draw. Try this:

```
fd(50)
color('red')
fd(50)
color('green')
width(10)
fd(50)
```

3. We can lift the pen up and put it down again, if we want to stop and start drawing.

```
home()
clear()
fd(100)
pu()
fd(100)
pd()
fd(100)
```

4. If you make a mistake, you can always undo the last command:

```
undo()
```

5. Let's try one final command before you start the challenges. This is how you tell the turtle to draw a circle:

```
circle(100)
```

Can you take a challenge?

• Can you draw a square with the turtle?

• How about a triangle?

• Can you draw a circle with a cross through it?

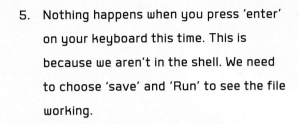

Loopy shapes

Saving your turtle

1. We have been writing all our commands in the shell up until now. This is easy to do, but it means that we lose all the fun pictures we have made when we close IDLE.

2. We can save our code, if we stop writing in the shell and use files instead.

3. In IDLE click on 'File' and then 'New File'.

File	Edit	Shell	Debug
New File			**⌘N**
Open…			⌘O
Open Module…			
Recent Files			▶
Class Browser			⌘B
Path Browser			
Close			⌘W
Save			⌘S
Save As…			⇧⌘S
Save Copy As…			⌥⌘S
Print Window			⌘P

4. Another window should open. This is where you can write all your code. We can start in the same way we did before:

```
from turtle import *
shape("turtle")
```

5. Nothing happens when you press 'enter' on your keyboard this time. This is because we aren't in the shell. We need to choose 'save' and 'Run' to see the file working.

6. You can do this from the menu bar like this:

File	Edit	Shell	Debug
New File			⌘N
Open…			⌘O
Open Module…			
Recent Files			▶
Class Browser			⌘B
Path Browser			
Close			⌘W
Save			**⌘S**
Save As…			⇧⌘S
Save Copy As…			⌥⌘S
Print Window			⌘P

Run	Options	Window
Python Shell		
Check Module		⌥X
Run Module		**F5**

7. The first time you save, you will need to name the file. Call it 'poly.py'.

A note on shortcuts

It's easier to use shortcut keys than always using the menus in files.

To save a file on Windows just hold down the 'ctrl' key and press the 's' key once.

To save a file on a Mac just hold down the 'cmd' key and press the 's' key once.

To run a file on Windows press the 'F5' key at the top of the keyboard.

On a Mac you can press 'F5' as well, but you may need to hold down the 'Fn' key at the same time.

8. Now let's try something fancy! Add in some more lines, so your code looks like this:

```
from turtle import *
shape("turtle")
for move in range(6):
    fd(50)
    lt(360/6)
```

9. Save your code and run it.

10. Do you see a hexagon being drawn? If not, check your code and try again.

11. You've just made your first loop in Python. The word 'for' starts the loop. The phrase 'in range (6)', makes the loop repeat six times.

A note on colons and spaces

The line of code that starts a loop must always end with a colon ':'

All of the lines underneath it will start with 4 spaces. IDLE puts these in for you, but if you delete them you can put them back in.

When you have finished writing the loop, remember to stop using 4 spaces at the start of the lines.

Loop Instructions that are followed more than once. It's easier to write a loop than writing out your code lots of times. You can use a 'for' loop to repeat some code a certain number of times or a 'while' loop to keep repeating the code until something happens, such as a variable changing to a certain number.

12. Let's try a different shape. Change your code so it looks like this:

```
from turtle import *
shape("turtle")
for move in range(5):
    fd(50)
    lt(360/5)
```

13. Can you see how the numbers in the code change the number of sides of the shape? An octagon has 8 sides. Try changing the numbers in your code to make an octagon.

Fun with 'for' loops

There are lots of things we can do with loops – why not try this:

1. Make a new file and call it 'star.py' (click on 'File' and 'New File').

2. Now add in this code. It uses a '**for**' **loop**, but this time the distance to move forward is stored as the variable 'size'.

```
from turtle import *
shape("turtle")
begin_fill()
size = 100
for move in range(9):
    fd(size)
    rt(160)
```

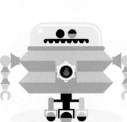

'**For**' **loop** Code which repeats instructions a certain number of times

3. This code makes the turtle move forward by one hundred and then turn by 160 degrees, and it does this 9 times.

4. Save and run your code to see what it looks like. What happens when you change the value of 'size'? Play around with your code and see what you can make.

5. Let's see if we can make it look more interesting with some different colours. Change your code so it looks like this:

```
from turtle import *
shape("turtle")
color("green","purple")
begin_fill()
size = 100
for move in range(9):
    fd(size)
    rt(160)
end_fill()
```

6. The 'color("green","purple")' line makes the turtle draw green lines with a purple fill. Remember that colour is spelt the American way: 'color'. Because programing languages are used all over the world, a standard way of spelling some words had to be chosen. American English is used for most languages.

7. The 'begin fill()' and 'end fill()' commands make the turtle fill in colour between the lines.

8. Have a play around with changing the colours, size, turn, and number of repeats. Can you make more interesting shapes?

9. Can you make your own loop that creates cool patterns and shapes? You can put as many lines of code into a loop as you want, just make sure that each line starts with 4 spaces. Try this one to start with:

```
from turtle import *
shape("turtle")
color("red","orange")
begin_fill()
for move in range(20):
    fd(120)
    bk(60)
    pu()
    rt(6)
    bk(50)
    pd()
    lt(24)
end_fill()
```

Fun with functions

1. Functions are a great way of reusing the same code over and over again. They are like the custom blocks you used in Scratch.

2. Create a new file and call it 'fun.py'.

3. We can start with a simple function to create a square:

```
from turtle import *
shape('turtle')

def square():
    for side in range(4):
        fd(100)
        rt(90)
```

Call Tell a program to follow the instructions in a function

4. Notice that like a loop, the function needs a ':' and then 4 spaces in front of each of the lines inside it.

5. If you run your code now, nothing will happen, because we need to call the function – we need to tell the computer to use the function code.

6. This is easy to do! We normally call a function by typing its name followed by (). Change the code so it looks like this:

```
from turtle import *
shape('turtle')

def square():
    for side in range(4):
        fd(100)
        rt(90)

square()
```

7. Run this code to see your square. If it doesn't work, carefully check your code – remember, all the best coders break their code as they learn!

8. Now we have a function to draw a square. We can call the function from inside a loop. Add a few lines to your code so it looks like this:

```
from turtle import *
shape('turtle')

def square():
    for side in range(4):
        fd(100)
        rt(90)

for times in range(5):
    square()
    rt(72)
```

9. See if you can make it look a little prettier. Try this to start off with, and then see where your imagination takes you:

```
from turtle import *
shape('turtle')

def square():
    for side in range(4):
        fd(100)
        rt(90)

color("purple","green")
begin_fill()
for times in range(5):
    square()
    rt(72)
end_fill()
```

Turtle illusions

This time we're going to make an optical illusion using our turtle. Once you're done, see if you can impress your friends with it.

1. Create a new file and save it as 'illusion.py'.

2. We can start with a few extra commands to set up our program. Try this:

```
from turtle import *
speed(10)
bgcolor("black")
width(10)
```

3. This sets our turtle to a faster speed, so the drawing doesn't take too long. It also sets the background colour to black, and the pen width to 10.

4. The first thing we want to do is draw a thick and very long line. Can you change your code so that it looks like this?

```
from turtle import *
speed(10)
bgcolor("black")
width(10)

def line():
    color("grey")
    fd(800)
    bk(2000)
    fd(1200)
```

5. Nothing will happen when you run the file, because we haven't called 'line()'. If you want to test out the code, try typing 'line()' into the shell (not into your file).

6. Now we want to use our line function to draw lots of lines. Change your code so it looks like this (turn over for example):

49

```python
from turtle import *

speed(10)
bgcolor("black")
width(10)

def line():
    color("grey")
    fd(800)
    bk(2000)
    fd(1200)

def lines():
    pu()
    goto(-300,300)
    pd()
    for times in range(7):
        line()
        pu()
        rt(90)
        fd(100)
        lt(90)
        pd()
```

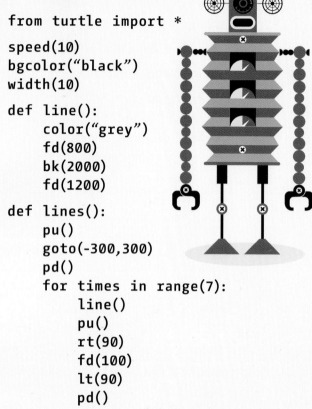

```python
def line():
    color("grey")
    fd(800)
    bk(2000)
    fd(1200)

def lines():
    pu()
    goto(-300,300)
    pd()
    for times in range(7):
        line()
        pu()
        rt(90)
        fd(100)
        lt(90)
        pd()

def grid():
    lines()
    lt(90)
    lines()
```

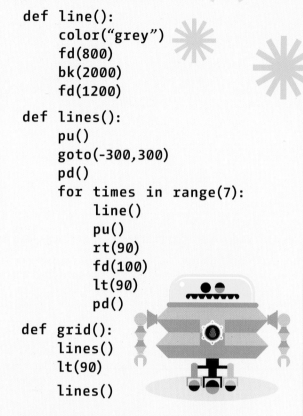

7. Here we move the turtle to the corner of the screen, and then tell it to draw our lines 7 times. After each line is drawn, the turtle moves down a little. Again, if you want to see the lines being drawn, save and run your file, then type 'lines()' into the shell.

8. Now we're going to use our lines function to draw a grid. Add a new function so that your code looks like this:

```python
from turtle import *

speed(10)
bgcolor("black")
width(10)
```

9. Save and run your code, then type 'grid()' into the shell, to make sure your grid is being drawn.

10. Now we're going to create a function to put dots in the grid. This will help create the visual illusion itself. Add a function to your code so that it is the same as the one below:

```python
from turtle import *

speed(10)
bgcolor("black")
width(10)
```

```
def line():
    color("grey")
    fd(800)
    bk(2000)
    fd(1200)

def lines():
    pu()
    goto(-300,300)
    pd()
    for times in range(7):
        line()
        pu()
        rt(90)
        fd(100)
        lt(90)
        pd()

def grid():
    lines()
    lt(90)
    lines()

def dots():
    color("white")
    pu()
    goto(-300,300)
    setheading(0)
    for i in range(7):
        for i in range(7):
            dot(20)
            fd(100)
        rt(90)
        fd(100)
        lt(90)
        bk(700)

grid()
dots()
```

11. This uses a 'for' loop inside another 'for' loop, so check that you have the correct number of spaces before each line. On the next line, 'dot(20)' adds a sized 20 dot onto the screen. The last two lines call our functions.

12. Run your code and see what happens. What colour do the circles look like to you? Ask somebody else to have a look at your optical illusion and see what they think!

Can you take a challenge?

- What happens to your optical illusion if you change the size of the dots? What happens if you change the colours of the lines?

- Have a look on the Internet for images of other optical illusions. Can you try and create one of your own? How about something like this?

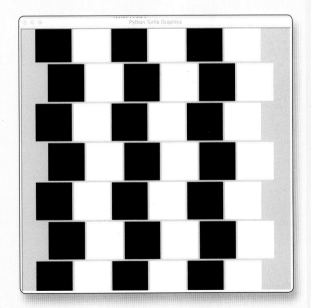

Fun with strings

What are strings?

In programming, the word string is short for "a string of characters". Characters are all the letters and symbols you can see on your keyboard (a-z, 0-9) plus others that you don't see like ♥ or ☺. So a string is just one or more characters put together. In Python, strings are always surrounded with double or single quotation marks. You can use either, but keep them the same on each line of code, like this:

```
"Hello World!"
'I love Python'
```

String
Sequence
of characters

Input and output

We can use Python to output strings. Let's have a go at making some of our own.

1. Open IDLE and create a new file.

2. Save your file as 'pippa.py'.

3. Now type this into your new file:

   ```python
   print("My name is Pippa the Python")
   ```

4. Save and run your file, and the words should be printed in the shell.

5. We can also get strings from the user, and save them as a variable. Try this:

   ```python
   print("My name is Pippa the Python")
   name = input("What is your name? ")
   print("Nice to meet you", name)
   ```

   User
   Person using a
   computer or program

6. When you save and run the file, the first line will be output to the shell. Then in the shell you can type your name, and Pippa should reply to you.

7. What if we want Pippa to say different things depending on who she is talking to? We can use 'if' statements to do this. We use a double equals sign (==) to see if "name" is equal to "Poly". In Python a single equals sign is used to set a variable, and a double equals sign is used to test if two things are the same.

   ```python
   print("My name is Pippa the Python")
   name = input("What is your name? ")
   if name == "Poly":
       print("You are an awesome coder,", name)
   else:
       print("Yuck,", name, "is a horrible name.")
   ```

8. You can change the name 'Poly' to your own name, and then save and run your code.

9. Try typing in your own name and then running it again, and getting a friend or someone in your family to type in their names.

Random replies

1. Let's make our code a little more interesting!

   Add in a line at the top of your program, so it looks like this:

```
from random import *
print("My name is Pippa the Python")
name = input("What is your name? ")
if name == "Poly":
    print("You are an awesome coder", name)
else:
    print("Hmm,", name, "that is not the name I expected.")
```

2. Now we can add some nice things for Pippa to say. We'll put the things to say in a list, which is surrounded by '[ ]'. Then we use the 'choice( )' command to pick a random thing from the list.

```
from random import *

praise = choice(["You are cool", "You are amazing", "You sound lovely"])

print("My name is Pippa the Python")

name = input("What is your name? ")
if name == "Poly":
    print("You are an awesome coder,", name)
else:
    print("Hmm,", name, "that is not the name I expected.")
```

3. Then we can use the nice things in Pippa's reply.

```
from random import *

praise = choice(["You are cool", "You are amazing", "You sound lovely"])
print("My name is Pippa the Python")
name = input("What is your name?")
if name == "Poly":
    print(praise,name)
else:
    print("Hmm,", name, " that is not the name I expected.")
```

4. Save and run your code to make sure it is all working.

5. Add some more nice things for Pippa to say into the list.

6. We can make Pipa reject people as well. Change your code so it looks like this:

```
from random import *

praise = choice(["You are cool",
"You are amazing", "You sound lovely"])
denied = choice(["Access denied", "You're not allowed here",
"Abort, abort"])
print("My name is Pippa the Python")
name = input("What is your name? ")
if name == "Poly":
    print(praise, name)
else:
    print(denied, name)
```

7. Save and run your code and then test it on yourself, your friends and family.

8. Add more random phrases to the list, to make it more interesting.

Rock, paper, scissors

1. We can use what we have learnt so far to make a game of rock, paper, scissors!

2. Create a new file and save it as 'game.py'.

3. We are going to need the random module again

```
from random import *
items = ["ROCK", "PAPER","SCISSORS"]
print("Welcome to rock, paper, scissors")
```

4. Save and run your game, to make sure it works so far.

5. Now let's find out if the player wants to choose rock, paper, or scissors.

```
items = ["ROCK", "PAPER", "SCISSORS"]
print("Welcome to rock, paper, scissors")
player = input("Choose rock, paper or scissors")
print("You chose",player)
```

6. Save and run your code. In the shell you can type your choice of rock, paper or scissors.

7. A computer can't tell that the word 'ROCK' is the same as 'rock' so we need to change the input so that it is all in capital letters. We can use the '.upper()' command to do this:

```
from random import *
items = ["ROCK", "PAPER", "SCISSORS")
print("Welcome to rock, paper, scissors")
player = input("Choose rock, paper or scissors").upper()
print("You chose",player)
```

8. Save and run your code again. If you type in 'rock' it should convert it to 'ROCK'.

9. But what if the player types something other than rock, paper, or scissors? We'll have to change our code so that it handles this!

```
from random import *

items = ["ROCK", "PAPER", "SCISSORS"]
print("Welcome to rock, paper, scissors")
player = ''
while player not in items:
    player = input("Choose rock, paper or scissors").upper()
print("You chose",player)
```

10. Here we are using a new loop called a 'while' loop. The line inside the 'while' loop will keep running until the player chooses something from the list. Save and run your code and then test it with the word 'rock' and then again with the misspelt word 'roc' to make sure it asks you to choose again.

11. Now the computer needs to make a 'choice()'. This code picks a random item from the list:

```
from random import *

items = ["ROCK", "PAPER", "SCISSORS"]
print("Welcome to rock, paper, scissors")
player = ''
while player not in items:
    player = input("Choose rock, paper or scissors").upper()
print("You chose", player)
computer = choice(items)
print("I choose",computer)
```

Dictionary
A way of organising data so that keys and values are linked together

12. Let's work out who has won the game! To start with, we need to write down the rules. We will use a dictionary for this. A dictionary is like a list, but it can store keys and values. You could use a dictionary to store peoples ages for instance {'Marc':10, 'Poly':7, 'Lisa':9} or to store words that rhyme {'cat':'bat','fall':'tall','red':'bed'}. The dictionary will tell us what beats what in this game. A dictionary is surrounded by { }

```
from random import *

items = ["ROCK","PAPER","SCISSORS"]
print("Welcome to rock, paper, scissors")
player = ''
while player not in items:
    player = input("Choose rock, paper or scissors").upper()
print("You chose",player)
computer = choice(items)
print("I choose",computer)

rules = {"ROCK":"SCISSORS","PAPER":"ROCK","SCISSORS":"PAPER"}
```

13. The rule dictionary has pairings of words inside it. "ROCK":"SCISSORS", tells us that "ROCK" beats "SCISSORS. PAPER":"ROCK" means that "PAPER" beats "ROCK".

14. To finish off we can use 'if' statements to see who has won the game. If the player and computer choices are the same (player == computer) then it s a draw. Otherwise the program can use the dictionary to see who has won:

```
from random import *

items = ["ROCK","PAPER","SCISSORS"]
print("Welcome to rock, paper, scissors")
player = ''
while player not in items:
    player = input("Choose rock, paper or scissors").upper()
print("You chose",player)
computer = choice(items)
print("I choose",computer)
rules = {"ROCK":"SCISSORS","PAPER":"ROCK","SCISSORS":"PAPER"}

if player == computer:
    print("We drew")
elif rules[player] == computer:
    print("You won")
else:
    print("I won")
```

Can you take a challenge?

- Can you use a variable to keep track of the player's score and a 'while' loop to keep the game running, until the player has scored 5 points?

- How about adding in more choices and rules? Look up the rules for Rock, Paper, Scissors, Lizard, Spock on the Internet.

15. Save and run the game. Well done! You have made your first Python computer game, and have made amazing progress.

Programming in the real world

What are hackers?

You've probably heard the word hackers before, but very few people understand what it really means. People think of hackers as nasty programmers who use their coding skills to break the law, to steal people's information, or sometimes even their money. This is because we often see stories in the newspapers or on the television, about criminals that have hacked into people's computers.

Hackers Experts at using a computer

Many programmers proudly call themselves hackers. They don't do anything illegal with computers, they just write code that does clever or unusual things.

Other programmers are very interested in writing code to break into computers or to take advantage of mistakes in other people's programs so that they can take control of a computer.

These hackers fall into two different groups:

Black hat hackers

Black hat hackers use their skills to break the law. They sometimes write programs that take control of other people's computers or steal information from computers. Sometimes they'll write programs called malware that can stop your computer from working, or make it behave in strange ways like opening websites that you didn't ask to be opened.

Black hat hackers Hackers who use their skills to commit crimes

Malware Computer programs that do bad things to computers

There are two main ways that a black hat hacker can access other people's computers. Sometimes people have simple passwords that are easy to guess, or they are tricked into telling the black hat what their password is. Another way of accessing somebody else's computer is to use what is known as a zero-day exploit. A zero-day exploit is a mistake that a programmer has made in their code, and because they didn't know about the mistake, they've had zero days to fix it. Until the code is fixed, a zero-day exploit can be used by a hacker to cause havoc.

Zero-day exploit Mistake in some software that the creator doesn't know about and has had zero days to fix

White hat hackers

White hat hackers have the same skills as black hat hackers but they don't break the law. Instead, when white hat hackers find zero-day exploits, they tell the programmers who made the software, so that they can fix the mistakes in their code. This stops black hat hackers using the zero-day exploit in the future.

Most companies will pay white hat hackers lots of

money to find zero-day exploits. There are even competitions for white hat hackers, with thousands of pounds in prize money for the ones who find the most zero-day exploits. White hat hackers are like the superheroes of the hacking world!

Indie and AAA games programmers

Many people first start learning to code because they want to make computer games. Maybe that's why you are reading this book right now! If you become a games developer, you might want to make either Indie Games or AAA Games.

Indie Games

Indie games developers work on their own, or with a few friends, to create their games. They do all the work themselves, from writing the code for the game, to creating the graphics, and thinking up the story. Indie developers don't work for any single company, so they are free to make whatever games they like for consoles, tablets, phones or PCs.

Some Indie games become extremely popular and can make the developers a lot of money. Sometimes the developers will give away their games for free, because they care more about the art of making games than making money. Indie developers might also sell just a few games to their fans. Probably the most successful and famous Indie game of all time is Minecraft.

AAA Games

AAA Games are made by large companies. These are the games that you see advertised on TV and that can often sell millions of copies. AAA Games are made by huge teams of people. There are programmers to write the code, artists to make the 3D characters and scenery, writers to create the stories, musicians to compose the music, designers to design the levels, and then other huge teams in charge of advertising and selling the game.

Programmers that work for AAA Games companies will often be in charge of one very small element of a game. They might be experts in creating realistic water, or creating the rules that decide how the non-player characters act, or even something as specific as how to make flags flutter in the wind.

What is Free and Open Source Software?

If you become a programmer you will be able to work on **Free and Open Source Software (FOSS)**. These are programs written by coders either on their own or with the help of lots of other coders. Free and Open Source Software is free for people to use, copy and share. Best of all, you are also allowed to have a look through the code and to make improvements to it.

FOSS is really important. Most of the websites you visit on the Internet are sitting on servers that run on GNU/Linux.

GNU/Linux Free and Open Source operating system used on many computers around the world

This is a FOSS group of operating systems and it is being improved every day by thousands of programmers from all over the world. Do you or somebody in your family own an Android mobile phone? That phone will be running lots of FOSS. Do you use Firefox as your web browser? This is also based on FOSS.

Lots of people and companies help to make FOSS. Some people do it for fun, others do it because they want to help the programming community, and others do it as their job.

A secret key

Encryption is a way of changing information so that nobody else can read it unless they have the secret key.

Imagine you wanted to send a friend the message:

"Meet me at the park at three."

but you didn't want anyone else to be able to read it.

Encryption Disguising data so that it is impossible to read without knowing how it has been disguised

You could use a simple method of encryption to disguise your message. For instance you could use a key of 5 and then move each letter of your message forward 5 letters in the alphabet, as shown here:

abcdefghijklmnopqrstuvwxyz

fghijklmnopqrstuvwxyzabcde

So:

"Meet me at the park at three"

would become:

"Rjjy rj fy ymj ufwp fy ymwjj"

If your friend knows the key is 5 then they could easily **decrypt** your message to read its real meaning!

Encryption used today is much more complicated than this method, which was originally used by Julius Caesar, the Roman Emperor, to send messages to his generals.

Decrypt Make encrypted data readable

This method, called the **Caesar cipher,** would be really easy to decrypt, just by trying all twenty six possible keys, and seeing which key made sense of the message.

Programmers now create methods of encrypting information that are so complicated, it is impossible to crack them without having the key. This is really important, especially when you are using the Internet. When you send messages back and forth on the Internet, it is really easy for another person (maybe a black hat) to see your message. This could mean that someone could see what you were doing when you were typing in your password, doing some shopping or using your bank. To stop other people being able to read the messages your computer sends out over the Internet, the information is usually encrypted.

Caesar ciper Way of encrypting words by replacing the letters with other letters

You'll know if you are using encryption on the Internet, because the bar at the top of your web browser will say https:// instead of just http://. You might also see a little padlock symbol like this, which tells you that you are using encryption:  https: .

Web development

Web developers make web pages that work in a web browser. Many web developers build web pages in a language called JavaScript. You can also build some basic web pages by coding in a language called HTML. HTML stands for Hypertext Markup Language. It's not a programming language, because you can't actually write programs with it. Instead, your web browser turns HTML into normal words and pictures that you can understand.

To make a web page, you are going to need to use a text editor. If you are using Windows then you could use Notepad. On a Mac, you could use TextEdit. There are other text editors that are even better though, so you might want to search for Sublime Text or Atom and download either of those instead. Remember to always ask an adult before downloading new programmes onto your computer; this helps to keep your computer healthy!

Operating system Software that manages a computer, such as Windows, OS X and GNU/Linux

1. Open up your text editor, make a new folder to save your web pages in, and then have a go at writing the following few lines:

```html
<html>
  <body>
    <h1>This is my first web page</h1>
    <p>This is a page all about me</p>
  </body>
</html>
```

2. Save your file as 'index.html' – don't forget the html ending! Have a look in the folder you have made, and double-click on your file to open it in a web browser. It should look something like this:

3. There are lots of tags that you can try out. Try adding these lines between your '<body>' '<body>' tags.

```html
<em>I'm learning how to code.</em>
<a href="https://www.codecademy.com/">
And here is a good site to learn
from.</a>
```

4. Save your web page and then have another look at it in your browser.

If you want to learn more about coding HTML there are lots of online resources to help you out.

Find out more

Snap!

If you liked Scratch then you'll love Snap! It is another programming language that is very similar to Scratch. You can have a look at Snap! by going to http://snap.berkeley.edu/ in a web browser. Snap! is a little more complicated than Scratch, but it is also more powerful – you can do more things with it.

Snap! Programming language similar to Scratch

Touch Develop

If you want to write code on a tablet or phone and build apps that will run on mobile devices, then you should have a look at Touch Develop. You can have a play with Touch Develop by creating an account at https://www.touchdevelop.com/app/. Touch Develop has two modes – a Scratch-like mode that lets you drag and drop blocks, and a mode that lets you write scripts like you did in Python.

Touch Develop Programming language similar to Scratch which is designed to be used on smartphones and tablets

Making games with Pygame Zero

If you want to make computer games, then you should have a look at Pygame Zero. You can get instructions for installing Pygame Zero and some tutorials by going to http://pygame-zero.readthedocs.org/. Start off by asking an adult to help you install it on your computer. With Pygame Zero you can make games that use graphics and images and respond to key presses and mouse clicks.

The Raspberry Pi

This isn't a pudding – the Raspberry Pi is actually a tiny computer that can help you learn to code. There are hundreds of resources online to teach you how to code on the Raspberry Pi and https://www.raspberrypi.org is a good place to start. The Raspberry Pi has input and output pins which allow you to connect all types of devices and electronic components. This means you can write code to do anything from turning on a few lights, to controlling a robot on the Internet.

Raspberry Pi Cheap, credit card sized computer, designed to help people learn how to program

Codecademy

Codecademy at https://www.codecademy.com is a website that can help you learn to code. There are lots of things to learn about on this website: you can learn more HTML and JavaScript if you want to learn about web development. You could also improve your Python skills or learn a new programming language like Ruby.

Code Academy Website that teaches you to code in many different programming languages

Pygame Zero Library that makes writing games in Python easier

Glossary

Algorithm Set of instructions to perform a task

Block Palette Area in the Scratch GUI that contains the blocks that can be used in a script

Black hat hackers Hackers who use their skills to commit crimes

Caesar cipher Way of encrypting words by replacing the letters with other letters

Call Tell a program to follow the instructions in a function

Characters Symbols such as letters, numbers and punctuation marks

Clones Copies of a sprite and all its scripts

Code Instructions written in a programming language that a computer can follow

Codecademy Website that teaches you to code in many different programming languages

Coding Writing code for a computer

Compiling Converting a program into a language that a computer can run

Custom block Scratch block that does a specific task

Debugging Testing code to find and fix mistakes

Decrypt Making encrypted data readable

Dictionary Way or organising data so that keys and values are linked together

Encryption Disguising data so that it is impossible to read without knowing the secret key (how it has been disguised)

'For' loop Code which repeats instructions a certain number of times

Free and Open Source Software (FOSS) Software that you are allowed to look at, change, use and share

Fractal Never ending and repeating pattern

GNU/Linux Free and Open Source operating system used on many computers around the world

Graphical User Interface (GUI) Screen that lets you click buttons, or choose items from a menu, usually using your mouse, trackpad or touch screen

Hackers Experts at using a computer

Input Data that is received by a computer program

Interpreting When a program is run by a computer, one line at a time

Loop instructions that are followed more than once

Malware Computer programs that do bad things to computers

Module Code that can be used in other programs to perform a task

Operating system Software that manages a computer, such as Windows, OS X and GNU/Linux

Passphrase Group of words that is easy to remember but hard for someone else to guess

Program Design and write code

Programs Collections of instructions that a computer follows to perform a task

Programmer Person who writes code

Pygame Zero Library that makes writing games in Python easier

Python Programming language based on typing text which is designed to be simple to learn and use

Raspberry Pi Cheap, credit card sized computer, designed to help people learn how to program

Scratch Programming language created for children that uses blocks of code which can be connected together to make programs

Script Small section of code, which can be as short as a few lines, or as long as hundreds of lines. In Scratch, a script is a collection of blocks that you have joined together.

Scripts Area Area in the Scratch GUI where blocks can be assembled into scripts

Shell Program that follows written instructions

Snap! Programming language similar to Scratch

Software Name for a computer program or collection of computer programs

Sprites Images used in computer games

Sprites Pane Area in the Scratch GUI where available sprites can be seen

Stage Area in the Scratch GUI where the game or animation can be seen

String Sequence of characters

Syntax The rules of a programming language

Syntax error Mistake in a computer program caused by not following the rules of the programming language

Touch Develop Programming language similar to Scratch which is designed to be used on smart phones and tablets

User Person using a computer or program

Variable Symbol or name that represents a value

'While' loop – Code which will keep repeating until something happens, such as a variable changing to a certain number

White hat hackers Hackers who use their skills to protect people

Zero-day exploit Mistake in some software that the creator doesn't know about and has had zero days to fix

Index